United States Presidents

John F. Kennedy

Paul Joseph
ABDO Publishing Company

visit us at
www.abdopub.com

Published by Abdo Publishing Company 4940 Viking Drive, Edina, Minnesota 55435.
Copyright © 2000 by Abdo Consulting Group, Inc. International copyrights reserved in
all countries. No part of this book may be reproduced in any form without written
permission from the publisher.

Printed in the United States.

Cover and Interior Photo credits: Peter Arnold, Inc., SuperStock, Archive, Corbis-
Bettmann

Contributing editors: Robert Italia, Tamara L. Britton, K. M. Brielmaier, Kate A. Furlong

Library of Congress Cataloging-in-Publication Data

Joseph, Paul, 1970-
    John F. Kennedy / Paul Joseph.
      p. cm. -- (United States presidents)
    Includes index.
    Summary: A brief biography of the thirty-fifth president of the United States.
    ISBN 1-56239-745-1
  1. Kennedy, John F. (John Fitzgerald), 1917-1963--Juvenile literature. 2.
Presidents--United States--Biography--Juvenile literature. 3. United States--
Politics and government--1961-1963--Juvenile literature. [1. Kennedy, John F.
(John Fitzgerald), 1917-1963. 2. Presidents.] I. Title. II. Series: United States
presidents (Edina, Minn.)
E842.Z9J67 1998
973.922'092--dc21
  [B]   97-43648
                                        CIP
                                      AC

Revised Edition 2002

Contents

John F. Kennedy

*J*ohn F. Kennedy was the thirty-fifth president of the United States. He was the youngest man ever elected president. And he was the first Catholic president. But he never finished his first term.

Kennedy served in the U.S. Navy during **World War II**. He was awarded a **Purple Heart**. In 1946, Kennedy was elected to the U.S. **House of Representatives**. Six years later, he became a U.S. senator.

The **Democrats** chose Kennedy to run for president in 1960. In a close election, he became president of the United States.

Kennedy took office at a difficult time. America was fighting against the spread of **communism**. Kennedy successfully led the country through the Cuban Missile Crisis.

On November 22, 1963, Kennedy was **assassinated** in Dallas, Texas. His vice president, Lyndon B. Johnson, became the new president. He carried out many of Kennedy's plans for the country.

John F. Kennedy

John F. Kennedy (1917-1963)
Thirty-fifth President

BORN:	May 29, 1917
PLACE OF BIRTH:	Brookline, Massachusetts
ANCESTRY:	Irish
FATHER:	Joseph Patrick Kennedy (1888-1969)
MOTHER:	Rose Fitzgerald Kennedy (1890-1995)
WIFE:	Jacqueline Lee Bouvier (1929-1994)
CHILDREN:	Three: 2 boys, 1 girl
EDUCATION:	Choate School, London School of Economics, Princeton University, Harvard University, Stanford Business School
RELIGION:	Roman Catholic
OCCUPATION:	Author, reporter
MILITARY SERVICE:	Ensign and lieutenant, U.S. Naval Reserve
POLITICAL PARTY:	Democratic

OFFICES HELD: Member of U.S. House of Representatives,
                                               U.S. senator

AGE AT INAUGURATION: 43

YEARS SERVED: 1961-1963, died in office

VICE PRESIDENT: Lyndon B. Johnson

DIED: November 22, 1963, Dallas, Texas, age 46

CAUSE OF DEATH: Assassination

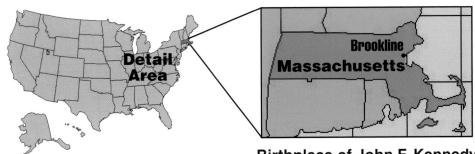

Birthplace of John F. Kennedy

Young Jack

*J*ohn "Jack" Fitzgerald Kennedy was born on May 29, 1917, in Brookline, Massachusetts. Jack's parents were Joseph Kennedy and Rose Fitzgerald Kennedy.

At the age of 25, Joseph became a bank president. Over the years, he made his fortune in the **stock market**. Rose's father was the mayor of Boston.

Joseph and Rose were married in 1914. Their first child, Joseph, Jr., was born in 1915. Jack was the second child. Seven other children followed: Rosemary, Kathleen, Eunice, Patricia, Robert, Jean, and Edward.

Religion, sports, and competition were a big part of the Kennedy children's lives. Joseph, Jr., dominated the family activities. Already his father was preparing him for a political career. Jack was content to grow up in his brother's shadow.

Jack attended private schools in New York and Connecticut. He was an average student. Jack's father encouraged him to play sports. But Jack was thin and did not excel at any sports. He was often sick while he was a student. He graduated from Choate School in 1935.

That year, Jack went to London to study economics. But he got sick and had to return home. In 1936, Jack entered Harvard University. He tried to succeed in sports but hurt his back playing football. But he improved as a student.

Jack's father became ambassador to Great Britain in 1937. The Kennedys moved to London, England. Jack worked for his father. He often visited other countries to observe important events. Then he reported what he had seen.

THE KENNEDY FAMILY:
(front row) - Robert and Jean;
(middle row) - John, Eunice, Joe Sr., and Patricia;
(back row) - Kathleen, Joe Jr., Rosemary, Rose, and Edward.

PT 109

*J*ohn Kennedy returned from London in 1939 to resume his studies at Harvard. That year, **World War II** began in Europe. Kennedy wrote a paper about the events leading to the war. His father got the paper published as a book. It was called *Why England Slept.* The book became a best-seller.

Kennedy graduated from Harvard with honors in 1940. Then he studied at Stanford Business School. In 1941, he volunteered for the U.S. Army. But they rejected him because of his weak back.

Kennedy spent the summer training with weights to strengthen his back. That fall, he joined the U.S. Navy. In 1943, he became a **lieutenant**. He commanded the torpedo boat *PT 109.*

One night that August, a Japanese destroyer rammed and sank *PT 109.* Kennedy re-injured his back. But he and his crew swam three miles to an island. Kennedy pulled an injured man along as he swam. Days later, Kennedy and his crew were rescued. Kennedy received two medals for his bravery. But he was sent home because of his back injury.

In 1944, Joseph, Jr., died when his navy plane exploded in flight. After Joseph, Jr.'s, death, Joseph, Sr., still wanted one of his sons to enter politics. He picked John. Soon, Joseph, Sr., began planning John Kennedy's political future.

Meanwhile, Kennedy had back surgery in 1945. He left the military that year. In 1946, Kennedy worked in San Francisco, California, and in London as a newspaper reporter. But the 1946 elections were coming. It was time to return to Boston to prepare for his new career.

Lieutenant John Kennedy during World War II

Congress

*J*ohn Kennedy ran for a seat in the U.S. **House of Representatives** in 1946. Joseph, Sr., used his political connections to promote his son's name. Robert Kennedy was Jack's campaign manager. Jack's sisters and brother traveled the country to promote his campaign.

John Kennedy made hundreds of speeches. He used his *PT 109* story to grab voters' attention. Kennedy easily defeated his opponent.

In **Congress**, Kennedy served on the Education and Labor Committee. He supported low-cost housing and better working conditions. And he supported the Truman Doctrine. It gave money to Greece and Turkey to rebuild after **World War II**.

In 1947, Kennedy traveled to Europe. In England, he became very sick. His doctors told him he had **Addison's Disease**. It was an illness he had since childhood.

Kennedy was glad to know why he was often sick. He took medicine to control the disease. He gained weight and felt better. In 1948 and 1950, he easily won re-election.

In 1951, Kennedy met Jacqueline Lee Bouvier. Jackie was a newspaper photographer and reporter. She was from a wealthy family, and was well educated. And she could beat Jack at word games at which he excelled. Jack found her intelligence appealing. The couple began their courtship.

In 1952, Kennedy decided to run for the U.S. Senate. He campaigned hard. And once again his family helped him. Kennedy defeated the popular **incumbent** by more than 70,000 votes.

As a senator, Kennedy helped pass several laws that were important to Massachusetts. And he voted for the St. Lawrence Seaway. It connected the Great Lakes to the Atlantic Ocean. Kennedy also voted to keep the **electoral**

Kennedy casts his ballot in the 1946 election—the first election in which he ran.

college. And he was committed to improving **civil rights**, raising workers' wages, and increasing defense spending.

On September 12, 1953, Kennedy married Jacqueline Bouvier. They had two children: Caroline and John, Jr. Another son, Patrick, died two days after his birth.

Kennedy was still suffering from back problems. In 1954, his doctors recommended a series of back operations. From October to February 1955, Kennedy remained in bed.

While he rested, Kennedy decided to write a book that he had been thinking about for years. The book was about eight of the most courageous senators in the nation's history. It was titled *Profiles in Courage*. It became a best-seller. The book won Kennedy the 1957 **Pulitzer Prize** for biography. And it made him a national **celebrity**.

In 1957, Kennedy started thinking about becoming president of the United States. He began by regaining his U.S. Senate seat in 1958. Kennedy won by nearly a million votes, the biggest victory in Massachusetts history. The huge win boosted Kennedy's confidence. Now it was time to start campaigning for the 1960 election for president.

Opposite page:
Jack and Jackie at
their wedding

The Making of the Thirty-fifth United States President

1917
Born May 29 in Brookline, Massachusetts

1935
Graduates from Choate; travels to London to study economics

1937
Father named ambassador to Great Britain; family moves to London

1940
Graduates with honors from Harvard

1946
Elected to Massachusetts House of Representatives

1952
Elected to U.S. Senate

1953
Marries Jacqueline Lee Bouvier on September 12

1958
Re-elected to the U.S. Senate

1960
Kennedy is elected president; son John is born

1961
The Bay of Pigs invasion; Berlin Wall is built

PRESIDENTIAL

John F. Kennedy

"And so, my fellow Americans: Ask not what your country can do for you, ask what you can do for your country."

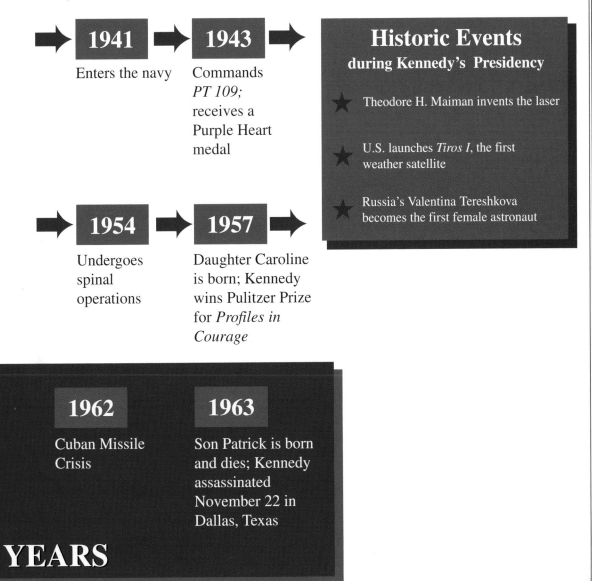

1941 → Enters the navy

1943 → Commands *PT 109;* receives a Purple Heart medal

Historic Events
during Kennedy's Presidency

★ Theodore H. Maiman invents the laser

★ U.S. launches *Tiros I*, the first weather satellite

★ Russia's Valentina Tereshkova becomes the first female astronaut

1954 → Undergoes spinal operations

1957 → Daughter Caroline is born; Kennedy wins Pulitzer Prize for *Profiles in Courage*

1962 Cuban Missile Crisis

1963 Son Patrick is born and dies; Kennedy assassinated November 22 in Dallas, Texas

YEARS

Election

*K*ennedy campaigned throughout 1960. Robert Kennedy was his campaign manager. Edward also was on his campaign team. Jackie made public appearances and gave speeches. Joseph, Sr., used his influence and power to help his son in any way he could.

Kennedy easily won the **Democratic** nomination. Senator Lyndon B. Johnson was chosen to run for vice president. The **Republicans** chose Richard Nixon to run for president. Nixon was the vice president of the United States.

In September and October of 1960, the two candidates met for a series of **debates**. For the first time in U.S. history, the debates were shown on television. Nixon looked nervous. Kennedy looked confident. Americans who watched the debates felt Kennedy had won.

The 1960 election was one of the closest in American history. Nearly 69 million people voted. Kennedy received only 120,000 more votes than Nixon. John Kennedy had become the thirty-fifth president of the United States.

John Kennedy (right) faces off against Richard Nixon in the first nationally televised presidential debate.

The New Frontier

*J*ohn F. Kennedy was **inaugurated** president on January 20, 1961. In his inaugural speech, he outlined his plans for the "new frontier."

President Kennedy believed that outer space was the new frontier. He wanted to put an American on the moon before 1970.

During this time, America's enemy was the **Communist** country the Soviet Union. The Soviets had already launched a spacecraft called *Sputnik*. America wanted to stay ahead of the Soviets. This competition was called the Space Race.

Another new Kennedy program was the Peace Corps. It would send American volunteers to help poor people in other countries.

Kennedy also wanted to create laws to stop **segregation** and **discrimination** in America.

Congress approved many of President Kennedy's plans. They included better social security benefits, higher wages for working people, and money and food for the poor.

When President Kennedy took office, the **Central Intelligence Agency (CIA)** was

Cuban dictator Fidel Castro

planning to invade Cuba. It wanted to overthrow Cuba's **dictator**, Fidel Castro. He had led a successful **rebellion** in 1959.

The U.S. government was not happy with Castro. He was a **Communist**. America wanted to stop the spread of communism throughout Latin America.

In April 1961, Cuban **exiles** invaded Cuba at the Bay of Pigs. The **CIA** helped plan the invasion. But Castro's army captured most of the invaders. President Kennedy traded food and money for the prisoners. He accepted the blame for the failed invasion.

Kennedy had more problems with communism throughout the world. In August, the Communist government of East Germany built the Berlin Wall between East and West Berlin. They wanted to stop people in Communist East Berlin from fleeing to West Berlin.

U.S. officials view the Berlin Wall from the West Berlin side.

In 1962, **Communist** China invaded India. President Kennedy sent weapons to India's army. At the same time, South Vietnam was fighting against Communist North Vietnam. Kennedy sent thousands of U.S. military advisers to help the South Vietnamese with their war.

In October 1962, Kennedy saw photos of Soviet nuclear missile bases under construction in Cuba. He announced that the U.S. Navy would block the coast of Cuba. The blockade would stop Soviet ships from delivering supplies.

Nikita Khrushchev, the Soviet leader, warned Kennedy that the Soviet Union would defend its shipping rights. A nuclear war might begin. But Kennedy held his ground. The Soviet ships reached the blockade, then headed back to the Soviet Union. Kennedy had won the showdown. This event became known as the Cuban Missile Crisis.

Kennedy feared that other Latin American countries might become communist. To stop this, he created the Alliance for Progress. It said the U.S. would help Latin American countries so they would not turn to communism. All Latin American countries, except Cuba, signed the agreement.

Soviet Premier Nikita Khrushchev

22

CHERRY PICKER

LAUNCH PAD WITH ERECTOR

LAUNCH PAD WITH ERECTOR

MISSILE READY BLDGS

OXIDIZER VEHICLES

FUELING VEHICLES

In 1962, a U.S. spy plane shot this photo of a Soviet-built nuclear missile base in Cuba.

The Seven "Hats" of the U.S. President

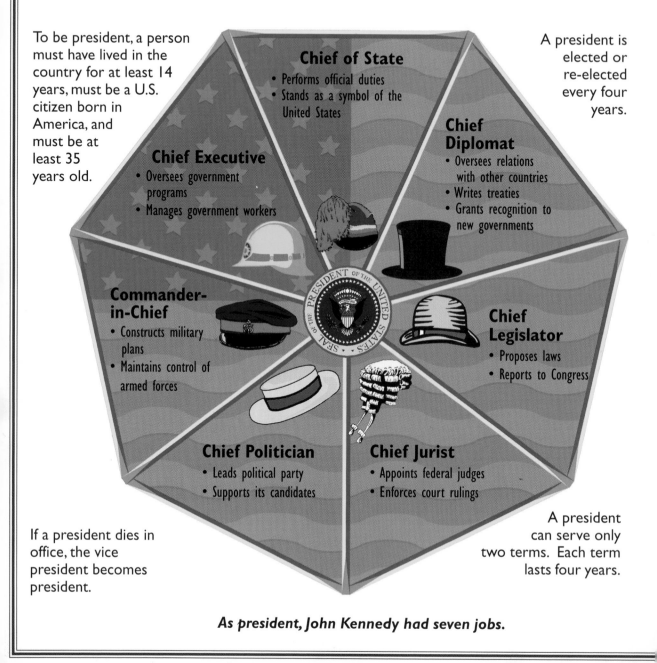

To be president, a person must have lived in the country for at least 14 years, must be a U.S. citizen born in America, and must be at least 35 years old.

A president is elected or re-elected every four years.

Chief of State
- Performs official duties
- Stands as a symbol of the United States

Chief Executive
- Oversees government programs
- Manages government workers

Chief Diplomat
- Oversees relations with other countries
- Writes treaties
- Grants recognition to new governments

Commander-in-Chief
- Constructs military plans
- Maintains control of armed forces

Chief Legislator
- Proposes laws
- Reports to Congress

Chief Politician
- Leads political party
- Supports its candidates

Chief Jurist
- Appoints federal judges
- Enforces court rulings

If a president dies in office, the vice president becomes president.

A president can serve only two terms. Each term lasts four years.

As president, John Kennedy had seven jobs.

The Three Branches of the U.S. Government

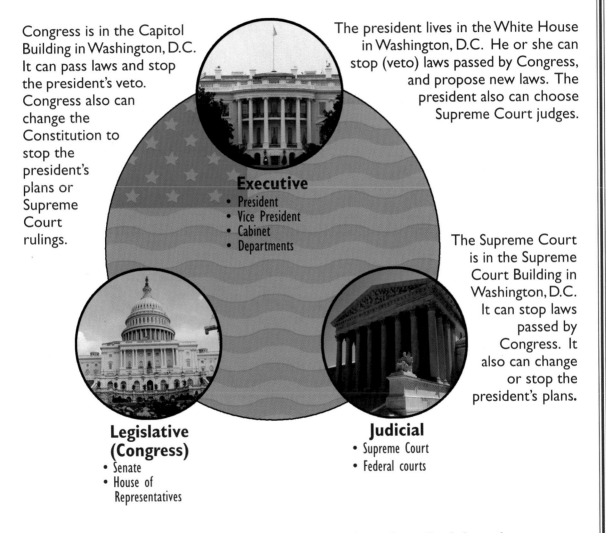

Congress is in the Capitol Building in Washington, D.C. It can pass laws and stop the president's veto. Congress also can change the Constitution to stop the president's plans or Supreme Court rulings.

The president lives in the White House in Washington, D.C. He or she can stop (veto) laws passed by Congress, and propose new laws. The president also can choose Supreme Court judges.

The Supreme Court is in the Supreme Court Building in Washington, D.C. It can stop laws passed by Congress. It also can change or stop the president's plans.

Executive
- President
- Vice President
- Cabinet
- Departments

Legislative (Congress)
- Senate
- House of Representatives

Judicial
- Supreme Court
- Federal courts

The U.S. Constitution formed three government branches. Each branch has power over the others. So, no single group or person can control the country. The Constitution calls this "separation of powers."

Dallas

*I*n 1963, Kennedy prepared for re-election. An important campaign stop was Texas, the home state of Vice President Lyndon Johnson. On November 22, the president and the first lady flew to Dallas on the presidential airplane, Air Force One.

The Kennedys paraded through Dallas in a convertible limousine. At about 12:30 in the afternoon, President Kennedy slumped over into his wife's lap. He had been shot through the head and throat. He died thirty minutes later. Lyndon Johnson took the oath of office on board Air Force One and became the new president.

Lee Harvey Oswald worked at the Texas School Book Depository building from which the shots were fired. Oswald was arrested for killing the president. But he denied his involvement. Two days later, Jack Ruby shot and killed Oswald as Oswald was being taken to another jail. Ruby was sent to prison for life.

OPPOSITE PAGE:

(Top photo) - The Texas School Book Depository in Dallas, Texas. The arrow marks the window from which the fatal shots were fired. Kennedy's car had passed by on the street below.

(Bottom photo) - Lee Harvey Oswald talks with reporters after his arrest for the assassination of John F. Kennedy.

The entire world was shocked at the death of President Kennedy. About 250,000 people passed by his flag-draped coffin to pay their last respects. Leaders from 102 countries attended his funeral. Jacqueline Kennedy lit an eternal flame at the president's gravesite in Arlington National Cemetery.

During his three years as president, John Kennedy faced challenges in Berlin and Vietnam. He also gave the nation a vision and a goal for future space travel. But he is best remembered for successfully leading the country through the Cuban Missile Crisis, and away from nuclear war with the Soviet Union.

A military guard leads Kennedy's flag-draped coffin from the White House.

Visitors view the eternal flame at John Kennedy's gravesite in Arlington, Virginia

Glossary

Addison's Disease - an illness that causes weakness, weight loss, and low blood pressure.

assassinate - to murder a very important person.

celebrity - a famous or well-known person.

Central Intelligence Agency (CIA) - a part of the U.S. government that gathers information about other countries.

civil rights - the rights of every U.S. citizen.

communism - a system where everything is run and owned by the state and given to people as they need it. It was seen as a threat because the Soviet Union, a communist nation, was an enemy of the U.S. after World War II.

Congress - the lawmaking body of a nation. It is made up of the Senate and the House of Representatives.

debate - a public talk about topics or questions.

Democrat - one of the two main political parties in the United States. Democrats are often liberal and believe in more government.

dictator - a leader who rules with absolute control and can be unjust or cruel.

discrimination - when people are treated differently because of the color of their skin.

electoral college - the group that elects the president and vice president by casting electoral votes. Members of the Electoral College are elected by popular vote—the vote of the people—in each state.

exiles - people who are not allowed to be in their own country.

House of Representatives - a group of people elected by citizens to represent them. They meet in Washington, D.C., and make laws for the nation.

inaugurate - when a person is sworn into a political office.

incumbent - the holder of a political office.

lieutenant - a naval rank above lieutenant junior grade and below lieutenant commander.

Pulitzer Prize - a prize given for outstanding achievement in writing.

Purple Heart - a medal given to any member of the military who is wounded or killed in action.

rebellion - when people fight against their government.

Republican - one of two main political parties in the United States. Republicans are often conservative and believe in less government.

segregation - to separate people based on their skin color.

stock market - a place where stocks and bonds, which represent ownership of businesses, are bought and sold.

World War II - 1939 to 1945, fought in Europe, Asia, and Africa. The United States, France, Great Britain, the Soviet Union, and their allies were on one side. Germany, Italy, Japan, and their allies were on the other side. The war began when Germany invaded Poland. America entered the war in 1941 after Japan bombed Pearl Harbor, Hawaii.

Internet Sites

www.abdopub.com

Would you like to learn more about President John F. Kennedy?
Please visit **www.abdopub.com** to find up-to-date Web site
links about President Kennedy and other presidents of the
United States. These links are routinely monitored and updated
to provide the most current and safest Web sites available.

Index